WALKING WITH GOD

ALISON FENNING

This book is dedicated to the five women who died during the Suffolk Murders and to those who survived.

Contents

Street Chaplain

Some people ignore those struggling with addictions. Few take the time to listen to the story of how a woman or a man comes to be in the situation they find themselves in. None of them planned prostitution or addiction as a career move. But somehow they find themselves trapped in a vicious circle and they can't see a way out.

Nearly a decade ago, Alison Fenning stepped into the world of some of these people in Ipswich, Suffolk. She offered non-judgemental friendship and a listening ear. At first she was mistaken for a Social Worker. While she occasionally provided practical help she was more concerned for the spirituality of the people she was meeting.

She became *'The Street Chaplain'*. Some of the women had done time and knew the prison chaplain was someone who could help, pray and advise. Back out on the street maybe The

Street Chaplain could do the same.

And so Alison began to make real friendships with women in the Red Light district of Ipswich. Along with her volunteers they spent long dark evenings kerb-crawling - not to abuse the women but to be a blessing to them. When the women were hurting she would pray for them there on the street, come rain or shine. On Valentine's Day she'd take them a rose. At Easter she'd give them chocolate. At Christmas a small gift-wrapped present. In these small acts of kindness, many of the women began to see the light of Christ.

Then in 2006 the Suffolk Murders rocked these new friendships. Girls she had spoken to a few days before were being found dead and appearing on the National TV News.

However, Alison stood firm and prayed and wept with the remaining women.

She held simple Bible studies on a Town Centre bench, in the shopping area, for small groups of girls and spoke of the love of Jesus. She held communion services in crack-dens.

And gradually the women, and a few men, began to believe that perhaps there was hope and a future in Christ.

Now the work switched to daytime and meeting for coffee and questions about spirituality like 'How do I do the God stuff?'

Women watched Alison lay hands on the sick and healing came. So they laid hands on their friends in Jesus' name and they got healed too. The Kingdom of God began to shine in the darkness. And now so many are asking, 'How do I do the God stuff?' that Alison has decided to share some of these conversations in this book.

Not all of her new friends are free of addictions yet but they are taking first steps in the faith.

In a series of 'letters' Alison encourages her readers to take a step of faith. She mentors us in the hard lessons she has leant in her walk with God.

When Alison joined the staff of RSVP Trust, I had no idea all this would happen. But I am so glad Alison joined us and felt free to be herself. She sometimes calls me 'Boss' but to be honest, I have learnt so much from Alison's walk with God that it never feels like that sort of arrangement.

I cannot recommend this book highly enough. If you are trying to walk with God on your journey through life, this is the book you need to read.

Don Egan
Director of RSVP Trust

one

Doing the God Stuff

Dear Lisa,

I am so thrilled that you feel you are connecting with God and seeing His inspiration in your life each day. I have decided to write to you each week about some things that will help you in this exciting new faith in God. Finally after many years of us spending time together chatting and praying about faith in God, you have discovered God and this faith is now your own.

I have prayed for you and others for many years, that the God I know, and am devoted to, would become the God of your life too. There is such a complete relief that settles on the inside of us when we know we are loved and accepted and we no longer have to walk through this life on our own.

A few weeks back I was asked to meet a friend of mine in a coffee shop early one morning. She had been reading a Bible someone had given her and she was excited and confused all at the same time. We sat down and then the questions began to pour out. The main one being 'How do I do this God stuff?'

I suddenly became aware that it is a brave new world we enter when we follow Jesus and, actually, there are not many people in our lives to help us navigate this new world. One day we suddenly bump into God and then we have to work through all the challenges of what it means to be a follower of Jesus and join his gang.

But his gang doesn't have a hard test to complete before we join. You don't have to prove yourself to him or to others. Joining the Jesus gang comes about through a prayer from the heart. My prayer was something like *'God help me! I can't go on anymore without you.'* Your prayer may have been a bit longer. But what really matters is that we call on God to help us, as we give our life over to him. The moment we do that, our inner God-life is activated.

The Bible calls Jesus' gang 'church' but that word just means a gathering of God's people. Jesus said he'd show up just for two or three.

The main thing is that you have called on the name of Jesus. That is what switches you on to God.

'Everyone who calls on the name of the Lord will be saved.'

Romans chapter 10: verse 13.

two

What just happened?

Dear Jade,

I remember thinking, I don't know what just happened? One day I was outside of God and now I am inside. I think I have decided to become a person who loves God and tries to follow the path Jesus has shown us. That's where I found myself one day after praying a prayer that went something like this.

Heavenly Father

Thank you for loving me and sending your Son to die for me. Today I give my life to you and I turn from my sinful life and ways and I ask you to come into my heart and live with me. I thank you that I am forgiven for all the sins I have ever committed. I receive your Holy Spirit as a seal on my life into eternity.

Amen

However, I am not sure I knew what any of

that prayer fully meant at the time. All I knew is what I believed – that there is someone upstairs (known as God), and, when I speak to him, things change and I feel peaceful. That's what praying this prayer did for me. It brought me a sense of peace and belonging.

I had been hanging around church since being born, having been christened and then occasionally taken to church by my parents. This had given me an opportunity to experience God before I really knew Him. I suppose that's God's goodness and kindness to me. I knew that God was a healer from a young age. Like you, I had been in meetings where I saw people healed and indeed I had felt the power / energy / presence - whatever word you prefer to use. But it took me years to accept that I wanted more than to just know about this God. Like others I wanted a proper relationship with Him.

In a relationship you get to understand and hear what another person is saying. In the Bible we read that God listens to us and then talks back. That's what I was after and now, as I write this to you, I have been living this way with God for eighteen years. So it is eighteen years since I cried out to God and then prayed a prayer making a vow to follow Him and pursue a life with the mark of God on it. Living with God is not always easy. It's a harder path but a more fulfilling one with an eternal outcome -

our life doesn't stop when we die. When we die then we will see God face to face and live with him forever.

If you're reading this and this is your experience too, then yes I would say that you have joined the world of church types, people who believe that God is real and that he is interested in their lives. By the way, they tend to call themselves Christians or followers of Jesus.

The great thing is you don't have to understand everything to have a relationship with God or speak to him. In fact, it is often easier to have a fantastic friendship with God if you don't think too hard about how this all works. Just keep living in the good of it and keep Jesus as the main focus of your faith!

three

God's Story

Dear Jade,

Having now connected with God, it would probably be a great help to know how this happened. So here is the God-story in a short understandable version. If you want to know the fuller version then I suggest reading the Bible, the collection of books about God.

'In the beginning' is a famous line found in the Bible in the book of Genesis, chapter one, verse one. It starts to tell the story of how God created the universe. Also it shows us that God has a family - the Holy Spirit and a son, Jesus Christ, who were all there in the beginning of time and have been present throughout Gods story.

In chapter two we notice that humanity begins with Adam and Eve. The first couple had an amazing friendship with God. Each day God came to speak to them. He advised them the best way to live and what to eat and what not to eat and gave them some work to do in his garden. Humans were the friends of God and very close to each other. Unfortunately this great friendship was heading for a painful divorce.

In chapter three we see Gods archenemy come to speak to Adam and Eve in the form of a snake (subtle and unseen until the last moment). The enemy of God is known as the devil or Satan. The devil has not always been God's enemy, as we learn from other books in the Bible. He was once part of Gods angelic gathering but he came to want to be above God and led a rebellion in the heavens, taking other angels with him as he was booted out of heaven.

We often think of the devil as a man with red horns but the Bible paints a different picture showing us what he was like before he led the rebellion and what happened as a result. the Bible shows us what he is up to now, trying to get us to rebel against God - same old thing really - drawing people into death and destruction through deception.

The importance of looking at this part of God's story is that we can see how God intended our friendship to be, coming to speak with us daily, giving us some work to do in his land and enjoying everything he created. The problem is that when the snake chatted to Eve, he put doubt in her mind and together with Adam they choose to join the rebellion against God - and like the devil they got booted out of the garden.

The garden is full of light and life. When humans joined the rebellion they swapped sides and went into the dark. So God had no choice but to let them leave as this is what they had chosen. But he gave them a gift when they left - he made them clothes because he loved them dearly. Maybe he feared for them as a parent as he knew that the life outside of the kingdom of light would be hard. God cursed the snake and vowed to make a way for his children and their descendants to come back into the garden and be free of the darkness.

So we see how the story began and the pain that God went through - the loss, the fear for those he loved, and a promise of a plan of action, to bring them back into the freedom of friendship with God, and to rescue them from being slaves of darkness. The Bible tends to use words like salvation, righteousness and justification and you may wonder what these mean. Well the Son of God, Jesus Christ, and his role in the story explains those big words.

More from the Bible
Ezekiel 28:12-17

John 8:44

John 10:10

2 Peter 2:4

Jude 1:6

four

Getting connected

Dear Jade,

Jesus is what Christianity is all about. God the Father had a plan since the beginning of time, to bring His Son into the world to rescue humanity from the corrupt works and eternal destination that the evil one had lined up. The devil's plan is revealed in the Bible way back in the Garden of Eden, where he comes and puts a lie into Eve's mind. His plan for each of our lives is to steal, kill and to destroy us. Often he will use our lives to destroy others too.

Following the lie of the devil brought a condition that has affected the entire human race since that time. The Bible calls it 'sin.' We could say that sin is really not living according to the promises of God but living by the lies of the devil. It will cause us to think, do and speak wrongly toward God and other people. This is why we have death, sickness, wars, hostility, envy, fights, and cruelty as part of the human race.

Sin will always separate us from God, as in him there is no sin but only love and faithfulness. So when we sin it is difficult for us to be with God. We will also find ourselves hiding from God due to guilt and shame. But there is some great news! God has provided a plan for us to step right back. This plan is activated by Jesus. God appointed him to be the Saviour of the world. When Jesus died, all human sin was placed upon him. This is why Jesus suffered. You can read about this in the places listed at the end of this letter to gain a perspective on this. Jesus came and suffered on our behalf so he could fix the broken relationship between God and us. Someone had to pay the price of sinfulness. If it wasn't Jesus it would have been us, seeing as it's our sin. That's why we look to Jesus in love as the one who reconnected us to God.

After the crucifixion of Jesus he laid dead for three days. The Bible says that in those three days a war was being fought, and Jesus went to the place of the dead and preached that he was going to be raised to life after three days. He took the keys of death away from the evil one and came back to life, fully victorious in that battle. Jesus is alive! So that when we surrender our lives to Jesus, and make him the boss of our life and follow his ways, we are reborn spiritually and become a child of God.

The book of Colossians reveals to us that God the Father has chosen to make Jesus the boss, or Lord, over all creation. Therefore, if Christ is the boss and Lord of everything, then we need to be in a relationship with him. It is only through Jesus Christ that we can approach our Heavenly Father. It is written in the gospels (Mathew, Mark, Luke and John) that Jesus said he was the Way, the Truth and Life and that no one comes to the Father except through him. Jesus is the source of forgiveness and eternal life and we are free of condemnation from the evil one when we live with Jesus.

The Bible reveals that we can only be in a relationship with God the Father is through accepting his Son Jesus as our Saviour, thereby turning our backs on a life without God and the things that displease Him - with our focus fully devoted to living our life with Jesus as Lord. This simply means we place Jesus in charge of our lives, letting his plan and purpose for us to come into being and allowing his teachings to direct our thoughts, challenging and gradually reforming our behaviour.

When we pray (speak to God) asking him to forgive us of our sinful ways and asking Jesus to come and live in our heart, bringing his influence and love to our world, the Bible teaches us that Jesus will come and be with us and never leave us.

John 14:23 Jesus replied, 'Anyone who loves me will obey my teaching. My Father will love them, and we will come to them and make our home with them.'

Rev 3:19- 21 19 'Those whom I love, I reprove and discipline; therefore be zealous and repent. Look, I stand at the door and knock; if anyone hears my voice and opens the door, I will come in to him and will dine with him, and he with me. He who overcomes, I will grant to him to sit down with me on my throne, as I also overcame and sat down with my Father on his throne."

More from the Bible

Genesis chapter 3

Isaiah chapter 53

Colossians chapter 1 verses 15-29

1 Peter chapter 3 verses 15-22

John chapter 14 verses 6

five

Slap your life on the cross

Dear Jade,

So then you will need to know about the importance of how Jesus died and in what way and then you will see how that affects us today. The cross is often talked about and is actually central to you in your journey of faith. As I explained in an earlier letter about getting connected to God through Jesus, we explored that Jesus actually died in our place so we can have our opportunity for relationship with God sorted. It is only because of Jesus that we can enter into the gift of eternal life plus other fabulous benefits. One of those benefits is through the way Jesus died on a cross and its relevance for today.

The Bible tells us that Jesus was put to death after being tortured on a wooden cross. The cross at that time was the most humiliating and painful death and was given to criminals who were executed for crimes. We can we think of it in terms of a completely innocent man executed for the crimes of humanity as Jesus is the only perfect born human to have ever walked the earth

'Since then we have a great high priest who has passed through the heavens, Jesus, the Son of God, let us hold fast our confession. For we do not have a high priest who is unable to sympathize with our weaknesses, but one who in every respect has been tempted as we are, yet without sin. Let us then with confidence draw near to the throne of grace, that we may receive mercy and find grace to help in time of need'

Hebrews 4:15-16.

Jesus was born to Mary who was a virgin - yep that's right, she had never had sex with a man until after Jesus was born. As we read the story of what happened in Luke, chapter one, we learn that God was actually the Father of Jesus and no, God didn't have sex with Mary but planted the seed of Jesus through supernatural means, the Holy Spirit - powerful stuff!

Every crime against God that we have ever committed, the Bible calls 'sin.' Jesus Christ chose to take on his own body the consequences of our sin - pretty amazing. So what would it mean for us if he had not done this on our behalf? Well, we would have had to suffer what Jesus suffered on our behalf when he died. That would be full separation from God and his presence. To see what Jesus did, read up below in 'Gods take on things.'

So the death of Jesus on the cross has great significance and power in our lives today. The cross represents the place where we can take any sin to Jesus, and confess it to him and be forgiven, and not separated from God. This does not mean that if we break the laws of our land or country we do not have to confess it or pay the price. We will still have to live with the consequences of our actions whilst on earth but in heaven the sinful action is no longer against your name in book of life.

So when we sin, breaking Gods laws, probably most days, it is important to realise that sin not only occurs through actions but in our thoughts and the words we say.

Jesus said, 'What comes out of a man is what makes him 'unclean'. For from within, out of men's hearts, come evil thoughts, sexual immorality, theft, murder, adultery, greed, malice, deceit, lewdness, envy, slander, arrogance and folly. All these evils come from inside and make a man 'unclean'.' Mark 7:20-23.

But we are able to have the burden of that taken away. We can be released from the horrible way it makes us feel as we hand it over to Jesus, at the foot of the cross. We can visit him whenever we need too. Being mindful in this way disciplines the heart and produces eventual change. Our transformation comes through Jesus working in our lives and it is not about us changing ourselves. Anyway, guess what? We wouldn't be able to do it ourselves. Once we came under pressure, the real us would come out to play, which is why we need a Saviour.

> *When we have sadness, anger or grief we can chuck that on the cross too. Jesus asked that we would – 'Come to me, all you who are weary and burdened, and I will give you rest. Take my yoke upon you and learn from me, for I am gentle and humble in heart, and you will find rest for your souls. For my yoke is easy and my burden is light.'*
>
> *Mathew 11:28-30.*

You will notice that, in life, many people come and promise to love us unconditionally and then end up letting us down. But Jesus is the only true loving Saviour who has our best interest at heart. That's why we love and follow him - we can trust him completely.

To obtain the benefits of what Jesus has done for us means that we must come to the cross daily and lay our lives down, deciding each day to pick up the way of the cross. By this I mean living God's way, which requires that we lay down our own selfish desires, impulses and behavior and embrace God's plan for our life. This happens through the activity of the Holy Spirit in our lives. As we are prayerful, the Spirit of God starts to transform our life but we also need practise living God's way until it clicks. Sometimes we have to choose to do the right thing and walk away from our destructive behavior patterns.

It is not an easy road to travel. The Bible says its a narrow way but we can choose to walk the narrow road as Jesus had gone ahead and walked that road himself. When he was born, he left his position in heaven and became fully human, choosing to walk in God's ways through the activity of the Holy Spirit in his life. That means it is possible for us and the only thing that would stop us is sin, and he has dealt with that problem already. So I wait with excitement to see the narrow road unfold each day for you as you continue your God journey. Don't ever give up because God has provided everything you need to make it. Remember when you screw up, deal with it quickly by saying sorry at the cross.

More from the Bible

John 19: 17-24

John 19:29-37

John 20:10- 23

Mathew 11:18-30

Luke 9:57-62
1Peter 3:13-22
Isaiah 43:25
Psalm 103:12

six

Guidance and power

Dear Lisa

How are we supposed to follow Jesus and do the things he did when He walked the earth? From a human perspective it is impossible. We notice that when Jesus was baptised in the River Jordon, an incredible thing happened. The heavens opened and Jesus saw the Holy Spirit come down in the form of a dove and land on him. This was accompanied by a voice from the heavens. This was God the Father's voice affirming his son, Jesus

'As soon as Jesus was baptised, he went up out of the water. At that moment heaven was opened, and he saw the Spirit of God descending like a dove and landing on him. And a voice from heaven said, 'This is my Son, whom I love; with him I am well pleased."

Matthew 3: 16-17

So Jesus did not do anything supernatural

himself until the day when the Holy Spirit came upon him. He led a normal life, living with his Mum and Dad and having a career as a tradesman. Being born as a jew he went to the temple and learned the scriptures. In the book of Acts, the first followers of Jesus were told not to do anything until the power from on high gave them power. In fact, John the Baptist, who baptised Jesus and many others, made a statement that he would baptise with water but that Jesus would baptise with the Holy Spirit and fire

> *'I baptise you with water for repentance. But after me comes one who is more powerful than I, whose sandals I am not worthy to carry. He will baptise you with the Holy Spirit and fire"*
>
> *Matthew 3:11*

When we are connected to Jesus through giving our life into his hands, and seeking to live his ways, a supernatural power is available to us. This power enables us to live the life more like Jesus.

When Jesus was walking the earth he was full of the Holy Spirit. This was God's gift to him to enable him to fulfill his purpose. The Holy Spirit is an unseen person – that's why he is called the holy 'spirit.' Jesus gives us the same opportunity to receive the gift of the Holy Spirit.

The Holy Spirit has been around since the

creation of the world. We first learn about his existence at the same time as God himself in Genesis chapter one. What we call the Godhead is made up of the Father, the Son (Jesus Christ) and the Holy Spirit. They all function together. Not one them functions without the other. We could say they operate as a healthy family in full agreement about all they do.

The Holy Spirit's function is very specific and can be found in the book of John chapter fourteen. He communicates to us the messages from the throne room. He convicts us of wrong-doing (sins) that we may need to repent of (change our thoughts, attitudes and actions) so we think and act differently. It is the work of the Holy Spirit to lead and direct us to God and to glorify God.

The Holy Spirit will not take God's glory or take praise that is due to the Father as the master craftsman in our lives. So we could say that his role is to be our helper in life. He does this by supernaturally coming to live on the inside of us - in the place where our own spirit is. Just as Jesus Christ was resurrected by the power of the Holy Spirit so we will as long as he lives in us.

There are signs given so we can know the presence of the Holy Spirit in our lives. He gives each person a gift. This gift it to used so that the church can function as Jesus did when he was walked on Earth. These gifts are given at the discretion of the Holy Spirit and can be read about in the scriptures below.

The gifts of the Spirit are to be used for good and not for evil. If we do evil in the presence of the Holy Spirit, we will find that he can not be part of those practices and we may sense a feeling of silence or loss of him. This is why it is vital to lead a godly life as much as possible and to repent immediately of sins that we do knowingly like bad thoughts we have or bad things we may say to people or behind their back.

A mark or a seal is set on our lives by the Holy Spirit that is recognised in heaven.

> *'And you also were included in Christ when you heard the message of truth, the gospel of your salvation. When you believed, you were marked in him with a seal, the promised Holy Spirit.'*
>
> *Ephesians 1:13*

This seal is a promise of eternal salvation and is given to those who choose to come home to God the Father, by accepting the ministry of Jesus Christ and his work on the cross. As Christ becomes the Lord of our life, the Holy Spirit acknowledges this act on our behalf.

More from the Bible

Matthew 3 verse 1- 17

Acts 2 verse 1-13

1 Corinthians 12: 1-31

John 14:1-28

John 15:26- 16:15

seven

Identity

Dear Jade,

When we look in the mirror we can see our reflection. We see the things we like and the things we don't. But our character is not based on what we look like or what style of clothes we wear. Our character comes from the inside of us and things we do and say come from our heart. The Bible tells us that 'God is concerned with looking at the heart but that human beings look at the body.' 1 Samuel 16:7. So we have a problem in society - people will always look at the outside and make a judgement about a person. This conditions us to do the same to ourselves. We look at ourselves and our past life.

The Bible tells us that once we have handed our lives into Gods hands a supernatural event occurs. 'We are born from the spirit of God,' John 3:5-7.

Jesus said, 'Truly, truly, I say to you, unless a man is born of water and the Spirit he cannot enter into the kingdom of God. That which is born of the flesh is flesh, and that which is born of the Spirit is spirit. Do not be amazed that I said to you that you must be born again.'

This means that we are a brand a new being or as the Bible puts it a new creation. Saint Paul writes to believers in a town called Corinth.

'Therefore, if anyone is in Christ, the new creation has come: The old has gone, the new is here'

2 Corinthians 5:17

This is great news and brings us hope that we have a future that is not dependent on our past. Our identity is now shaped by God.

The search for our identity comes to us all at some point in our life. We look for our history through what our grandparents did and where did they came from. We try and build a picture to see where we fit in and maybe gain a sense of our heritage. So we begin to define ourselves through other people's lives and experiences. This is great for some who may like what they find but for others it maybe painful and not something that we want to identify with at all, and certainly not define our future through what we discovered.

The Bible reveals that we have a history already that was designed and formed in heaven by God himself. In the book of Jeremiah, God comes to him and says, 'Before I formed you in the womb, I knew you, before you were born I set you apart. I appointed you as a prophet to the nations.' Jeremiah 1:4-6.

In Psalm 139 we learn that King David had the understanding that God was the designer of his life. Have you ever thought that you were designed by God? He is our heavenly Father. When we begin to think about God as a Father it would make perfect sense to me that he knows about each one of us.

Interesting to note that there appears to be a book that God holds in heaven with all our names in and our days on earth are marked out - all good things we will do and places we will go, maybe a picture of how we will look and who we will live alongside in our lives. The only thing that will destroy the things in the book would be sin, which we now have an answer for as explained in a previous letter. This book was written and designed before the foundations of the worlds, meaning that not one of us is a mistake. If you are alive, that's Gods plan and you are his idea. The book of life is also mentioned in the New Testament in Revelation 17:8.

If God is the Father and designer of our lives making us his idea before we were conceived, and our names were written in the book of life before we were born! Then we are his sons and daughters. We no longer have to be worried about who we are or feel hopeless but we can live in the reality of our true identity. We can explore and tap into what God has written in the book of life about us. We can move on and live out of true identity

As sons and daughters of God we become co-heirs with Jesus,

> . *'The Spirit himself testifies with our spirit that we are God's children. Now if we are children, then we are heirs - heirs of God and co-heirs with Christ, if indeed we share in his sufferings in order that we may also share in his glory.'*
>
> *Romans 8:16-17*

Jesus said to his followers 'I am the Way, Truth and the Life. No one can come to the Father except through me.' John 14:6. Jesus is the way back home to meet the father. He is the Way to God, the Truth of God and the Life of God.

The Father is waiting for us to sit with him, waiting to reveal his love and kindness toward us, waiting to unveil our true identity. This love is so powerful and genuine that nothing can come between us and God once we have relationship with Him. Paul writes in the book

44

of Romans 8: 38 -39 'For I am convinced that neither death nor life, neither angels nor demons, neither the present nor the future, nor any powers, neither height nor depth, nor anything else in all creation, will be able to separate us from the love of God that is in Christ Jesus our Lord.' At times we will need to hold on to this promise until it becomes firm in our mind and heart. Throughout the Bible, God reveals his love toward us, 'But God demonstrates his own love toward us, in that while we were still sinners, Christ died for us.' Romans 5:8.

Walking in your True Identity

What you repeatedly do communicates to people who you are. We become known by what we do and how we behave. In other cultures, what we do is not as significant as who your ancestors were and what tribe you were from. Neither theory is right or wrong, just different ways of interpreting the world we live in and the values we hold.

So how do we start walking in our true identity set by God? Well I would say if you start to practice living the life Jesus talks about, in Matthew, Mark, Luke and John, that is going to help a lot. You will begin to notice you think and act differently as you study and do what

Jesus teaches. Then we are truly following his ways. Jesus spent his life showing how to live God's way. So we have the Bible as a guidebook to advise us, then we practice until it becomes a natural habit. The Holy Spirit also helps in this transforming process. In our own strength we would not be able to do it but, as long as we stay connected to the life of God, the Spirit will help us. Jesus said 'As the Father loved me, I also have loved you; abide in my love' John 15:9.

This is where church can be a benefit and give you somebody to help mentor you in the process of change. Some days we will revert back to the old self and maybe think it's not working. But we have to remember we have an enemy - the devil - whose aim is to 'kill, steal and destroy' our lives. (John10:10) He will come and whisper things like 'It's not working', 'There is no God', 'You make the choices you want', and so on just like he spoke to Eve in the Garden. The enemy comes as a smooth talking liar, so we must be on our guard as he roams around looking to take us out. This is where we need a mentor or group of people to ask questions of. Someone who will encourage us not to give up and go back. In my experience, the more we encounter God the more we know his love on the inside. And we can't go back because we love him in return.

Walking in your true identity is based not on head knowledge but on in an intimate friendship with a living loving God. So I would say, spend time getting to know this loving God, through reading, prayer, and being around other people who are on the same journey. Let God show you how to walk with him. True identity brings hope, security and ultimately freedom. But false identity keeps us hopeless and bound.

'Do not let your hearts be troubled. Trust in God; trust also in me. In my Father's house are many rooms; if it were not so, I would have told you. I am going there to prepare a place for you. And if I go and prepare a place for you, I will come back and take you to be with me that you also may be where I am. You know the way to the place where I am going."

Thomas said to him, 'Lord, we don't know where you are going, so how can we know the way?'

Jesus answered, 'I am the way and the truth and the life. No-one comes to the Father except through me. If you really knew me, you would know my Father as well. From now on, you do know him and have seen him.'

Philip said, 'Lord, show us the Father and that will be enough for us.'

Jesus answered: 'Don't you know me, Philip, even after I have been among you such a long time? Anyone who has seen me has seen the Father. How can you say, 'Show us the Father'? Don't you believe that I am in the Father, and that the Father is in me? The words I say to you are not just my own. Rather, it is the Father, living in me, who is doing his work. Believe me when I say that I am in the Father and the Father is in me; or at least believe on the evidence of the miracles themselves. I tell you the truth, anyone who has faith in me will do what I have been doing. He will do even greater things than these, because I am going to the Father. And I will do whatever you ask in my name, so that the Son may bring glory to the Father. You may ask me for anything in my name, and I will do it.

If you love me, you will obey what I command. And I will ask the Father, and he will give you another Counsellor to be with you forever - the Spirit of truth. The world cannot accept him, because it neither sees him nor knows him. But you know him, for he lives with you and will be in you. I will not leave you as orphans; I will come to you.'

John 14: 1-18

As long as we keep living with Jesus then our new identity will become established in us each day. The Spirit of truth will guide and direct each step of the way.

Below are some Bible verses to read and think about by reading and pondering them until they become a truth in your head and heart. Maybe underline them in your Bible.

I am with God
I am a child of God (John1:12)
I am a part of the true vine, a channel of

Christ's life (John15:1,5)

I am Christ's friend (John15:15)

I am a son or daughter of God: God is spiritually my Father

(Romans 8:14,15; Galatians 3:26; 4:6)

I am joint heir with Christ, sharing his inheritance with Him

(Romans 8:17)

I am a member of Christ's body (1Corinthians12:27; Ephesians 5:30)

I am united to the Lord and am one spirit with Him (1Corinthians 6:17)

What God says about me:

I am a slave to righteousness (Romans 6:18)

I am enslaved to God (Romans 6:22)

I am righteous and holy (Ephesians 4:24)

I am chosen by God, holy and dearly loved (Colossians 3;12; 1Thessalonians 1:14)

This is who Jesus makes me:

I am a new creation (2 Corinthians 5:17)

I am one of God's living stones, being built up in Christ as a spiritual house (1 Peter 2:5)

I am a temple - a dwelling place - of God. His Spirit and his life lives in me (1Corinthians 3:16; 6:19)

I am not condemned because I am in Christ Jesus (Romans 8:1)

I am more than a conqueror through Christ (Romans 8:37)

I am helped by God and can receive mercy (Hebrews 4:16)

I am asked to be like Jesus!

I am destined to be like Jesus (Romans 8:29)

I am a child of light and not of darkness (1Thessalonians 5:5)

I am a partaker of Christ; I share in His life (Hebrews 3:14)

I am the aroma of Christ (2 Corinthians 2:15)

I am the enemy of the devil (1Peter 5:8) and His works

I have access to Gods wisdom (James1:5)

I am born of God so the devil cannot touch me (1John 5:18)

eight

Make the call

Dear Matt,

To pray is really important. Though prayer we connect directly with our heavenly Father. It is a central and vital part of working out our relationship with Him. Jesus has given us access to the Father through the work of his death and resurrection. Before Jesus Christ came to earth, the nation of Israel was not able to pray directly to God but needed a priest to offer prayers and sacrifices. But thanks to Jesus we now have access to God directly and therefore need to treasure this gift by using this provision for our lives.

I think of prayer as simply making a phone call to God - speaking to him and listening to his voice giving us direction for life each day. Any problems, fears, or decisions we may have, we can chat through with God and wait for his response. We can also pray for other people and ask God for his help. Prayer is the place where we can say thank you, at the end of the day, for God's provision in our lives.

Often prayer is easier if we get on our own and have a bit of quietness and space, otherwise we can get distracted and then never make the call. I tend to pray when I am driving or out running. You don't need to sit in a room all alone, just pray as you go about everyday activities. That way, we can pray throughout the day, meaning we continually connect with God.

What we may find, as we intentionally lead a prayerful life, is that we are changed on the inside. God uses the time we spend in prayer to blend his character into our character. This is a lifelong journey of change as ultimately we are being transformed into the glory of God. Simply meaning that we begin walking in his ways and thinking his thoughts. We begin sounding and looking like a child of God. We often look like our human parents and inherit their genes. So as we are connected strongly to God through an active relationship, we will start to look and sound and think like him as we allow him to Father us.

I encourage you to develop a personal prayer life but also to go to prayers in a church or chapel setting. You will find this really helpful as it will help to model how to pray and it also helps us to never give up when we feel it's not working right now. Praying with people of faith will bring the presence of Jesus into the mix immediately. Jesus told his followers 'Whenever two or three are gathered I am there in the midst of you.' When you pray, be yourself. Don't try and use the right words but speak from your heart to God. Remember 'God looks at the heart' so he wants to hear from your heart.

Prayer is what will bring a breakthrough for you in any area of life so it is really important to do it as often as you can. The Bible says that when we pray 'His eyes and ears are open to hear' (1 Chronicles 7:14-15). In those days it was connected to a specific place - in a temple building - but now we who choose to follow Christ and have given our lives to him, are the place where God's presence lives. That temple is now a human being - you and me and all the other millions of followers. That's why we can pray anytime and anywhere. God is on the inside of us waiting to hear from us his people. Makes it pretty cool and exciting really.

More from the Bible

Revelation 3:20

Psalm 34: 15

Mathew 6: 5-15

Ephesians 6:18

I Thessalonians 5:16-18

James 5 : 13-18

Revelation 8 verse : 1-5

Luke 18: 1- 7

nine

Read the book

Dear Jade,

As we have chatted so many times about you wanting to start to learn about the Bible and God and where to start, I needed to write to you about the background to it, so you can crack on with your desire to learn and be helped through engaging with God. Every time I sit and read I like to think that I am hearing God speak to me through his words and thoughts laid out in the Bible.

The Bible was written by people under the inspiration and direction of God. It reveals the story of God and humanity. Therefore the Bible is also called 'the word of God' His words to humanity through the ages, since the creation of the world and mankind until the story ends with God fully making everything come good, so we end up at the beginning again.

The Bible reveals many things. God's love toward us being one and his good thoughts toward the people who accept his son Jesus Christ and who seek to follow Him. It is full of stories of people who fail in life, really messing up. In other words, real people with major problems and character flaws, and how God still loves them and has a plan for their life, helping them through the darkest of times. Therefore it brings hope and confidence that we can trust God to turn any situation around for good.

As the Bible is full of God's words it is a very powerful book. It is alive and active in our lives everyday if we allow it to be. As we come to the Bible we can read it, say it aloud, meditate on the words, therefore changing our thoughts and actions through it, as we allow the Bible to be a source of guidance in any situation. As a consequence we will observe how God's words can transform our lives and help us to live a more fulfilled and purposeful life as we journey home toward the Father and heaven.

If we think we don't really have what it takes or that we are not good enough, the Bible helps us to see that we are a prime candidate for God's plan coming to pass in our lives. Time and again we read that it is not about following the rules but about letting the words of God reform and change our minds and hearts through a living and active relationship with the God of the Bible.

How we read the Bible is vital. It is full of different styles of writing and yet it holds the story and history of God's people and some individuals up and downs of life. Then there are books of wise ways to help in this life. Then there are the books of Jesus and the recordings of his life, followed by the story of his first followers and how they followed him and took the message of him as Saviour of the world and spread it across other countries. The important thing to remember is that as God's voice is clearly heard through the Bible. That is what makes it holy and something to be treasured and read.

Jesus Himself was familiar with the words of God his Father and he used them when he himself was tempted by the devil in the desert.

Then Jesus was led by the Spirit into the desert to be tempted by the devil. After fasting for forty days and forty nights, he was hungry. The tempter came to him and said, "If you are the Son of God, tell these stones to become bread."

Jesus answered, "It is written: 'Man does not live on bread alone, but on every word that comes from the mouth of God.'"

Then the devil took him to the holy city and had

*him stand on the highest point of the temple. "If you
are the Son of God," he said, "throw yourself down.
For it is written: "'He will command his angels
concerning you, and they will lift you up in their
hands, so that you will not strike your foot against a
stone.'"*

*Jesus answered him, "It is also written: 'Do not
put the Lord your God to the test.'"*

*Again, the devil took him to a very high mountain
and showed him all the kingdoms of the world and
their splendour. "All this I will give you," he said,
"if you will bow down and worship me."*

*Jesus said to him, "Away from me, Satan! For it
is written: 'Worship the Lord your God, and serve
him only.'" Then the devil left him, and angels came
and attended him."*

Matthew 4:1-11

What you may notice is that Jesus knew
these words and then used them when he was
under pressure. I always think this is a great
example to follow in times of pressure or when
you are trying to breakthrough in life in some
area. When we hear what God says we can hold
that thought in our minds and speak them out
when challenged.

How to read the Bible

The Bible refers to scripture as 'living and
active' (Hebrews 4:12) and that's due to God's
voice being all over it. God's voice is powerful
and can change situations, bring freedom on the

inside to our emotions, and comfort us, bringing wellbeing through security. Some times when I am under pressure or sensing insecurity starting to rise in me, I gently calm myself by reminding my mind of Gods word 'I can do all things through Christ who strengthens me.' (Phillipians 4:13) Then, before long, my confidence and security returns as I am reminded I am not alone in any struggles any more but I have a Great High Priest - Jesus - who I can gain strength from.

In other words, Gods truth filters into my mind and drops into the heart, bringing peace and harmony to my wounded soul. Inner healing occurs and I can move forward. Incredible when we take a moment to reflect on that gift that God has given us, meaning we can hear his voice daily, if we choose to listen for it.

Where to start

As with anything that brings hope and love to us we often push it away or don't access it frequently enough. Often we only visit the Bible in times of desperation, then wondering why it doesn't seem to work for us. I often think it is like medicine that will work well if we take a dose everyday, especially if all this is new to us. Like anything we won't know it all on day one but we grow into things over a period of time.

So where do we begin? Most people tend to turn to the front but remember it is not one book but a collection of 66 books. So one project we could do is to read the Bible cover to cover but also read a smaller book with in it maybe one chapter a day or a few verses a day and then think about what you have just read for the rest of the day.

I would recommend starting with the book of Mark and thinking about the life of Jesus and what he had to say, maybe make notes as you read and notice things that excite you as that maybe God's voice speaking to you. Then ask how does this affect me today? Once you have thought it through it's a great time to pray and have a chat to God about those things. For some people the beginning of the day works well. For others, evening is better. Try and find a space each day to connect with the Bible and hear God's voice for your life and you will start to see change, hope, peace and inner strength come.

More from the Bible
2 Timothy 3 16
Psalm 119:105- 111
Deuteronomy 11: 18
Colossians 3 : 16

Romans 15 : 4

Joshua 1: 8

Matthew 16:16-20

Acts 2 : 42-47

1 Peter 2: 1-10

ten

Let it go

Dear Jade

One of the harmful diseases we can pick up and carry around with us is bitterness. It will bring harm to us and to those around us. God's nature is to forgive. God has no bitterness, only the ability to forgive. You can read more about his character in the next chapter.

We humans find forgiveness one of the toughest challenges to act on. But, because of Jesus, we have a place to go that helps us when all the rubbish stuff that we do or others do to us gets on top of us, rather than making our hearts and minds corrupt with bitterness and getting offended - which only ever leads to revenge and that in turn produces negative behavior. In other words what's on the inside becomes visible to the world around us.

God requires us to drop all those who hurt us into his lap and let him deal with them in due time, I am talking about the practice of forgiving people.

It is often very difficult to know what people mean when they say 'Give your problems and resentments to God.' Easier said than done in some situations, when the wound has gone deep. I read something recently though that was really helpful, that a better way of saying it is to 'drop it or let it go'. See the problem as being held in a your clenched fist, open your fist and drop the problem and let it go as it falls to the ground. See Jesus catch it and let him deal with it. We can get so caught up in the situation around us that we become obsessed with that one thing instead of being focused on the now. Fortunately for me I am a big picture thinker, so I tend to think about life through the lens of the whole of my life span rather than the little bumps from day to day. But sometimes the day to day bumps and knocks seem too painful.

As I write this I am sat in a coffee shop and all around me there are conversations of people recounting problems, who has hurt them and what they are going to do to get them back, revenge seems to be the flavour of the day. We do seem intent as human beings to pick up grudges along the path of life and be determined to nurture them like babies. We talk about 'Nursing a grudge.' That's why they grow bigger. No wonder so many people are tired and depressed in our society. Just overhearing them is enough to get you down. But God knows that holding grudges will lead to our own downfall if you hold it for long enough. It will bear some ugly fruit, becoming destructive to you and those around you.

Once we have experienced Gods forgiveness in our lives then we are able to offer it to someone else. Now we know what it looks and feels like to be forgiven. It's difficult to do if you have never experienced it yourself. The Bible speaks very strongly that if we don't forgive others then we will not be forgiven by God 'But if you do not forgive others their sins, your Father will not forgive your sins' (Mathew 6:15). In other words, we can not expect to live a double standard and get away with it. That's fair enough when we think about it. It can be difficult to let things go before we are ready though. But we can begin to prepare ourselves by speaking to God the Father in advance. We may say something like 'God those people (or situations) really hurt me and its very unfair but I will need to forgive them as its still hurting me and I don't want to remain angry or afraid. So please help me in my heart and enable me to let it go.'

The Bible says 'If we claim to be without sin,

we deceive ourselves and the truth is not in us.
If we confess our sins, he is faithful and just and
will forgive us our sins and purify us from all
unrighteousness. If we claim we have not sinned, we
make him out to be a liar and his word is not in us.'
(1 John 1: 8-10)

By now I can hear you saying 'That's so
unfair!' But remember that we are on a journey
to lay down our lives and pick up the ways of
God. Jesus has shown us how to do this. Did
he not ask God to forgive those who falsely
accussed him and had him beaten and tortured,
and strung up on a cross and left to die?

Jesus said, 'Father, forgive them, for they do
not know what they are doing.' (Luke 23:34)
So we have to follow Jesus and sometimes
you may need to keep asking God to help you
forgive people until you wake up one day and
realise there is no longer a heavy burden trou-
bling you. Your heart and mind have become
clear. Forgiveness is an action and not a feeling,
so looking for a feeling first is the wrong way
round.

We have the choice each day whether to
let things go or hold onto them. The problem
comes when you hold on to grudges and then
those people who hurt you or the situations that
didn't go your way, are still having an impact
on your life even though it is a past event. It
will always be better for us to forgive so that

we can move on to the next chapter of our lives rather than keep going over the old one.

More from the Bible

Matthew 6:12-15

Matthew 9: 6

Matthew 18:21-35

Micah 6:8

John 20: 21- 23

Philippians 3: 13-14

Philippians 4:13

Peacemaker

'Blessed are the peacemakers, for they will be called children of God.' Mathew 5:9

One of the most powerful lessons I ever had in forgiveness was from when we did night outreach into the red light district in Suffolk UK in 2005. I had promised to take a woman we had become friends with to visit her parents graves. They had both been addicts and died when she was young. Yep you have already guessed what happened next - I forgot!

Thinking she would never speak to me again or at least verbally kick off at me I was shocked when she came over and just said 'We are OK you and I. I was upset but its all OK between us now. I just need you to know that.' Right there and then I received forgiveness. That was all before I had the chance to say sorry!

The fact that she had forgiven me was unbelievable but could I now dig deep enough to forgive myself as well? The fact that we are human beings with free will, desires and emotions can sometimes keep us locked in a prison of unforgiveness. The consequences can affect either us or others, meaning we can miss out on moving forward and living in the provision of freedom for our hearts and minds that God has granted.

I wanted to share this story with you for two reasons. Firstly, to show that we all mess up and can hurt others often unintentionally, but also the gift she gave that day will stay with me forever and I really treasure her forgiveness toward me. I experienced it so now I know what it looks and feels like. Now I can give that same gift to others and watch them be free from the burden of guilt, shame and condemnation.

As humans we are created to carry the presence and nature of God and are therefore able to make quality choices as Jesus did when he encountered conflict and disappointment. I always take great comfort knowing that Jesus experienced many malicious acts against him and came out free on the other side. What I notice through reading the gospel stories is that rejection, beatings, false accusation to name a few happened a lot and that the response of Jesus, and later his followers, came from the presence of God on the inside.

> *God's nature is found in Exodus 34:5-7 'Then the LORD came down in the cloud and stood there with him and proclaimed his name, the LORD. And he passed in front of Moses, proclaiming, 'The LORD, the LORD, the compassionate and gracious God, slow to anger, abounding in love and faithfulness, maintaining love to thousands, and forgiving wickedness, rebellion and sin.'*

Also the New Testament confirms God's nature.

> *'But the fruit of the Spirit is love, joy, peace, forbearance, kindness, goodness, faithfulness, gentleness and self-control. Against such things there is no law. Those who belong to Christ Jesus have crucified the flesh with its passions and desires. Since we live by the Spirit, let us keep in step with the Spirit.'*
>
> *(Galatians 5:22-25)*

The fruit of his Spirit enables us live as true representatives of God's kingdom. Without having an active friendship with God, through the work of Jesus and by the power of the Holy Spirit, we will not be able to display the fruit of his Spirit. So there is a challenge straight away for us to keep developing and investing time into our friendship with God to walk in His ways.

God wants us to walk daily in practicing the

gift of forgiveness. Firstly, so we can be free and feel good each day. Free of the anger and bitterness that often takes root and shows up in our actions. And, secondly, that others can experience the love of God through us.

In Matthew 18:21- 35 we find the story of an unforgiving person.

'Then Peter came to Jesus and asked, 'Lord, how many times shall I forgive my brother or sister who sins against me? Up to seven times?'

Jesus answered, 'I tell you, not seven times, but seventy-seven times. Therefore, the kingdom of heaven is like a king who wanted to settle accounts with his servants. As he began the settlement, a man who owed him ten thousand bags of gold was brought to him. Since he was not able to pay, the master ordered that he and his wife and his children and all that he had be sold to repay the debt. At this the servant fell on his knees before him. 'Be patient with me,' he begged, 'and I will pay back everything.'

The servant's master took pity on him, cancelled the debt and let him go. But when that servant went out, he found one of his fellow servants who owed him a hundred silver coins. He grabbed him and began to choke him. 'Pay back what you owe me!' he demanded. His fellow servant fell to his knees and begged him, 'Be patient with me, and I will pay it back.'

But he refused. Instead, he went off and had the man thrown into prison until he could pay the debt. When the other servants saw what had happened, they were outraged and went and told their master everything that had happened. Then the master called the servant in. 'You wicked servant,' he said, 'I cancelled all that debt of yours because you begged me to. Shouldn't you have had mercy on your fellow servant just as I had on you?'

In anger his master handed him over to the jailers to be tortured, until he should pay back all he owed.

This is how my heavenly Father will treat each of you unless you forgive your brother or sister from your heart.'

Elsewhere Jesus told Peter to forgive 70 times 7 - meaning lots and from the heart. There is emotion attached to forgiving. As a forgiver or the forgiven either way it will have an emotion about it and that emotion will feel good, as forgiveness brings freedom back to us. Freedom not to be offended, angry, sad or grieved but rather to be accepting and loving. This produces happiness that we are all secretly wanting.

When we fail to forgive ourselves it will result in shame, guilt, remorse and regret, leading to low self - esteem which may have consequences of isolation, anxiety and ultimately depression. These toxic emotions can cause pain and discomfort to us and affect people who are involved with us. Forgiveness can heal our emotions, creating an ability to love others and self again restoring deep peace of mind and heart and a sense of joy. How do u know if you have forgiven? It may be different for each of us but for me what were painful events, words or people are a mere memory that no longer causes strong reactions. Also we may notice that we are not going on about things, people, places, events or situations anymore with an attitude of injustice.

Reflections

If you are in a place to start moving forward (you may not be yet and that is alright, you will know when you are) but if you are then you could use the reflections below.

What grudges known and unknown do you hold in your mind and heart?

Can you find the compassion in you to let go of the people, places, events and situations?

What does it feel like to be free from those things?

Can we find it in ourselves to speak to God today about those things and trust him to deal with the issues around them?

Can we find it in heart to forgive others and ourselves? It may not be like the story that happened to me. It may not be confronting a person. It could be developing a state of mind really more than anything. Beginning by accepting the forgiveness of God through Jesus and then extending that out to others.

Jesus explained that those who that have been forgiven much, forgive much as love pours out of them toward others. He uses two powerful stories as an example that forgiveness keeps no records of wrongs.

'When one of the Pharisees invited Jesus to have dinner with him, he went to the Pharisee's house and reclined at the table. A woman in that town who lived a sinful life learned that Jesus was eating at the Pharisee's house, so she came there with an alabaster jar of perfume. As she stood behind him at his feet weeping, she began to wet his feet with her tears. Then she wiped them with her hair, kissed them and poured perfume on them.

When the Pharisee who had invited him saw this, he said to himself, 'If this man were a prophet, he would know who is touching him and what kind of woman she is-that she is a sinner.'

Jesus answered him, 'Simon, I have something to tell you.'

'Tell me, teacher,' he said.

'Two people owed money to a certain moneylender. One owed him five hundred denarii, and the other fifty. 42 Neither of them had the money to pay him back, so he forgave the debts of both. Now which of them will love him more?'

Simon replied, 'I suppose the one who had the bigger debt forgiven.'

'You have judged correctly,' Jesus said.

Then he turned toward the woman and said to Simon, 'Do you see this woman? I came into your house. You did not give me any water for my feet, but she wet my feet with her tears and wiped them with her hair. You did not give me a kiss, but this woman, from the time I entered, has not stopped kissing my feet. You did not put oil on my head, but she has poured perfume on my feet. Therefore, I tell you, her many sins have been forgiven-as her great love has shown. But whoever has been forgiven little loves little.'

Then Jesus said to her, 'Your sins are forgiven.'
Luke 7:36-48

The art of practicing forgiveness

1.   Check what comes out of your mouth: who are you talking about? Is it uplifting? Or are we constantly bad mouthing others and talking about the offensive action?

2.   Repent: consciously decide to settle in your heart that you are going to put it to bed.

3.   Pray that God will help you to have the ability to forgive like he does.

4.   Practice forgiving the person. Can you see yourself acting differently around them? Can you see yourself doing something kind for them taking no credit for it? It's a great sign that you're walking in forgiveness.

One other thing to say, if someone has been abusive or assaulted you physically, mentally or emotionally in some way, it will be a long process for you to come to the place where you are able to forgive in your heart, and God knows that level of suffering and he feels all the pain and sorrow on your behalf and will work with you regarding healing from those events. But what that doesn't mean is that you let them back in your life or that you remain silent about that abuse. You need to report it. When someone has committed a crime they still need to pay the consequences for that crime, even if you have forgiven them, in your heart. Forgiveness is a deep heart and mind issue that may require some help from a therapeutic perspective too.

Give yourself a break

I once met a man in Rwanda whose wife had been killed by another man. They were together in the same room - sat right next to each other smiling. As one man stood up to say he had taken the life of another person and that he was very sorry and admitted the hurt and pain he had caused (he had served prison time for this crime) then the man sat next to him stood up and accepted his apology as it was his wife the man had killed. They shook hands and began to sing freedom songs, as is custom in their land. They also have a custom of providing restorative justice. This is where the offender does an act of kindness toward the victim's family

- like building them house. So forgiveness in this way has a practical response and well as a heart one.

I was amazed and blown away by what I was witnessing. For the first time in my life I truly saw the possibility of what forgiveness looks like but I also saw the happiness and freedom it produced in both people, acknowledging that only God could make this possible. The Bible tells us that 'what is impossible with man is possible with God.' (Mark 10:27) I am sure we can all think of situations where we can't imagine being able to give or receive forgiveness.

Corrie ten Boom was a Dutch Christian who, along with her father and other family members, helped many Jews escape the Nazi Holocaust during World War 2. She and her family were sent to a concentration camp for this. During this time the Nazi soldiers killed all her family. It was in that dark place that she learned the power of forgiveness.

After the war she was able to speak all around the world about her experiences and the God who helped her often speaking about forgiveness and God's love. She forgave the Nazi soldiers who had put her family to death.

Whilst reading one of her books, *He Sets the Captives Free,* I noticed she refers to visiting an

African prisoner who was struggling to forgive. Her advice was to 'forgive people otherwise we won't be forgiven.' A difficult phrase to say and receive but one that Jesus taught.

'But if you do not forgive others their sins, your Father will not forgive your sins.'
Matthew 6:15

Maybe the biggest challenge we face as we go through life is to forgive ourselves when we mess up in thoughts, words or actions. Messing up will happen most days if we are honest with ourselves but don't despair as the prognosis for us is good!

Thanks to Jesus we have access to the love of God through the ministry of the Holy Spirit in our lives. If we hold onto sadness over our failings we are heading into resentment, bitterness and landing up on the step of self-hatred that can cause all sorts of issues. The Bible requires us to 'love others as we love ourselves' (Luke 10:27) The command is there to love yourself. If we do not consider this truth we will find it hard to love others as we can only give what we have received. We are often happy to hear God's kindness towards us but then beat ourselves up every day.

Loving yourself is a requirement from God because our body, mind and soul are the temple where he lives through the Holy Spirit in our lives. Therefore we should not despise the place where God lives. As we have mercy towards others we must also allow God's mercy to touch ourselves.

In extending forgiveness toward ourselves we must first get rid of the illusion in our minds that anyone of us is perfect. Newsflash: there is no such person apart from Jesus who was or is perfect and sinless. On the outside they may look or sound perfect but on the inside all around the world people are the same and in need of transformation. So we must stop striving for that false goal and stop trying to fix ourselves. It is the ministry of the Holy Spirit in our lives that transforms us. So we need more intimacy with God through prayer and stillness, not false unachievable goals in our lives.

Love is an action or attitude, so we may need to change our thinking regarding self-image, honouring the temple (oneself) where the Spirit of God lives when we have forgiven ourselves. The prayer below is the prayer that Corrie ten Boom prayed with the African man. You may want to say it and reflect on it yourself.

> *'Thank you, Jesus, that you have brought into my heart God's love through the Holy Spirit. Thank you, Father, that your love in me is stronger than my hatred.'*

By praying and reflecting on those words myself, I realised I have the ability and desire to forgive others and to forgive myself. It is God's work in my heart and his love is a gift that he gave to me. Therefore I must forgive myself as I forgive others. That is mercy in action. Remember the story at the beginning of the Rwandan man who offered forgiveness and the other man who received it. The outcome was relief and happiness. As we begin to forgive ourselves, we begin to experience deep relief in our souls, and happiness comes as an expression of the relief.

So give yourself a break and be kind to yourself let Gods love extend to you as well as outward to others.

ten

Give it away

Dear Matt,

Once we believe in Jesus and have invited him to be Lord in our life, something happens on the inside of us. God is now living with us each day through the presence of his Holy Spirit. This is powerful and we begin to want to share God's love with others as he becomes the best news ever and what was impossible becomes possible with God.

We all share what's going on for us. We see it every day as people meet up for coffee and just chat about what's happening. If we think back for a moment about how we got to hear about God, often it's because someone shared their story with us.

God has always had an agenda to make himself known. He is our long lost Dad. So as humans we join him in communicating his story through sharing ours story which has God in it. This plan has been on God's heart since the book of Genesis. God spoke to a man called Abraham and asked him to go. He sent him on a mission to move to a new area to share about the God he knew and connecting with people around him. Jesus in the Bible is still asking us to go. (Matthew 28:19-20) So we know that it is part of God's plan that we go and connect with those who have not met Jesus yet. We also see from reading the book of Acts, in the Bible, the first followers of Jesus lived the same way as he did and saw amazing things.

We can learn from the reading the Gospels that Jesus moved around and brought the Kingdom of God to peoples attention by healing the sick, teaching about the Kingdom, calling people into freedom from captivity, bringing hope and justice where needed, and feeding the poor. In other words, Jesus revealed God's heart and love for humanity. As we go we should be doing the same. We can start right now by praying for the people around us, at work or whom we meet up with regularly, and seeking to be kind and generous with everyone we meet. As we go we will find that not only are other people connected to God's love and power but also that we grow in our understanding of our faith.

More from the Bible

Philemon 6

Micah 6: 8

Matthew 28: 16-20

Luke 10: 1-20

1 Peter 3:16

eleven

Get in with the crowd

Dear Lisa

The word 'church' simply means 'the gathering of the people of God' and traditionally this is known to be on a Sunday. But when we read the Bible in depth, it refers to the church as the bride of Christ and the body of Christ, implying it is something very precious and something to be nurtured. When we have a loving relationship with Jesus we are to walk the same path as he did, loving others, hence the term 'body'. We are now the hands and feet whilst Jesus is the head or director. Just as went about doing good, full of the Holy Spirit, so should we follow in his steps.

'You know of Jesus of Nazareth, how God anointed Him with the Holy Spirit and with power, and how He went about doing good and healing all who were oppressed by the devil, for God was with

When we follow Jesus and make him Lord of our lives, then we have God's Spirit on the inside (we become the temple of God's Spirit). A body functions with purpose in some way, walk, talk, think, act and so on. So when the Church meets together, which can be anytime where two or three people are gathered, what happens is that the presence of the Kingdom of God is seen and shines out like a light on a hill, calling others to join them.

To be part of a community of believers is what Jesus modeled in the gospels and how the first followers lived in the book of Acts. We can read how a community worked in Acts chapter 2, they broke bread (took communion) to remember Jesus as he told us to, they prayed and shared all their things with each other doing the work of God - healing the sick, helping the poor, setting free those oppressed by the devil. As Jesus went around with the first followers and together they did the work of God, so as church today we do the same things as Jesus taught his followers. It is not a monument to the past but a living group of people who bring the kingdom of God to be made known and seen. The church carries the power of God with them wherever they go.

So I hope you will be able to see that the Church is much more than attending a Sunday service. The service is part of what a church will do as the gathering together as the people of God. A service facilitates our praise of God though song, praying and an opportunity to hear the Bible spoken with practical advice from the preacher.

The Bible says that we should not give up meeting together. This is because we will each pass through many things in our lives and there is strength in numbers. We will not get disheartened as we are feeding our spiritual life. When we are discouraged we have friends to help us through those times. Isolation occurs when we disengage from anything in life and that's when we are vulnerable to being picked off by the devil that roams around looking to stop and destroy our relationship with God. Also by meeting together we are confirming our identity as the people known to live as part of the Kingdom of God - something for the world to see, feel, and touch - enabling them to find God as we have.

More from the Bible

Matthew 16:16-20

Acts 2: 42-47

1 Peter 2: 1-10

Ephesians 4 : Chapter 5 verse 33

twelve

Being generous

Dear Matt

God has been generous with us. He has given us the gift of life and of being in a relationship with himself. The Bible reveals that none of us are here by mistake. We are God's design and even our names were chosen by Him before our parents even thought about us. He gave us our life.

'For you created my inmost being;
you knit me together in my mother's womb.
I praise you because I am fearfully and wonderfully made;
your works are wonderful,
I know that full well.
My frame was not hidden from you
when I was made in the secret place,

when I was woven together in the depths of the earth.

Your eyes saw my unformed body; all the days ordained for me were written in your book before one of them came to be.'

Psalm 139:13-16

God's nature is one of compassion, love and generosity. He is generous through and through. He is always looking to get provision to us if we have a vision for something that will help others. Once the human race was in deep need, we had become disconnected from God and the only way back to God was through the giving an offering that would be of great value and cost.

So God chose to provide the way back to himself by giving up his Son as an offering to carry the weight of offences that we as humans carry. In other words, he became our Saviour and our way back to God the Father. That is one big gift he gave to us.

So, as an expression of our love and faith toward God, we can give an offering from the heart. This can be through giving money or time or a skill to be used for the Kingdom of God, as an act of devotion. It will not buy you salvation or a relationship with God but it will reveal our hearts towards God.

The Jewish people who lived under the old

agreement with God used to give a tenth of what they gained in the year back to God as laid out in the laws of that time. But now after the death of Jesus we are under a new agreement. The laws have not changed but are now fulfilled by Christ our Saviour who took the punishment for breaking the laws as we would struggle to keep them.

Instead we live those laws seen in the light as the principles of God, or the ways of God. So whereas before it was law or duty to give a percentage of financial gain, now it is a heartfelt response, as Jesus now asks us to lay our lives fully down and be ready to love our neighbour as our self, and to love God with all our heart. What we have is God's grace (ability) living on the inside of us, so we can be ready when Jesus asks us to follow him, and give out of having nothing to give sometimes. But the Holy Spirit will give you a little jolt when he wants you to act and help someone in this way. I can remember when I started out doing ministry with RSVP. I turned up with a car that leaked petrol and £50 in my pocket with no promise of getting paid. I chose to live by trusting God that he would supply all my needs as I was doing what he had put on my heart. Three things happened.

Firstly, I didn't tell anyone about my need.

Secondly, a woman from the new church I started going to came and handed me an envelope with £200 inside, saying God had told her to give it to me. And thirdly, an elderly lady had died and decided to leave a large amount to the charity so that lump sum enabled me to begin ministry. So God does provide when we are faithful in our hearts toward Him.

As I have received, I also understand that I must be generous with what I have myself and often distribute finance or goods to where God is leading me each year. We are called to bless others because we have been blessed by God. It is like a cycle of giving and receiving that goes round and that way we are provided for. I think people in Africa understand this principle. They have nothing but still give out of their nothing and live another day still praising God for his love toward them. We can learn a lot from their amazing faith.

So as God gives to us we too should begin to be like him in nature by giving back to God and others. Everything we have belongs to God according to the Bible, as he owns the universe and created everything we are given. The reason we are blessed with homes, money, cars, and relationships is so we can give to others by acts of kindness when needed, just as Jesus did. Let us have an attitude of generosity to God and to others. When we live like this we are living as a giver, like God.

More from the Bible
Matthew 6:19-24
Luke 10: 27-37
Galatians 6 : 7
2 Corinthians 9: 6
Mark 12: 41-44

thirteen

Heading out

Dear Matt, Jade and Lisa

As you head out on your journey - walking with God - there are two main points I would like to leave with you. One is living by faith and the other is expecting miracles as you walk. I have learned many lessons whilst walking with God, which I may write about in another series of letters to you. But these two are the most important ones as you move around, and they go together.

As followers of Jesus we do live by faith. The Bible says 'The righteous shall live by faith.' (Romans 1:17) We are 'the righteous' once we have a relationship with God. Faith just means believing something you can't physically see. So we can't see God but something within us draws us to search for him until we find him. When we pray for people we are praying in faith to an invisible God and yet we believe he is there. (Romans 12:3) 'Faith is a gift from God that is activated when we are connected to God and are listening and responding.' Contrary to popular teaching, faith is not mental delusion, presumption or self-deception, but a work of the Holy Spirit and the Word of God.

What is Faith?

The Bible calls us to live by faith and not by sight. Most of the time we live by sight, believing circumstances and situations as they come to us. But when God is involved on the inside of us, we get to live according to his promise and by faith in that promise. The Bible is full of promises to us, as God's people, and those promises are to be seen fulfilled in our lives in the correct season of our lives. In other words, they are an unseen promise that one day becomes seen.

Hebrew 11:1 says, *'Now faith is the assurance of things hoped for; the conviction of things not seen."*

How do we do faith? We begin by searching out the promises of God in the Bible. You can underline the promises so you can see them. For instance, in the Bible it states that we will not stay babies in our faith but become mature believers. So to see this become true in your life, I would recommend you begin to pray the promise - asking God to teach you his ways, which will lead you to becoming mature in your faith.

The Bible plants the promises in our hearts and the Holy Spirit grows the seed of that promise so we must remind God of the promises. 'Faith comes by hearing and hearing comes through the word of God' (Romans 10:17) So as we spend time with God, reading the Bible and listening in prayer, faith will come and God's voice will come with it bringing, healing, wisdom and direction for our everyday lives.

Faith produces inner assurance, dependency on God, trust and obedience. If we live by faith and not sight we will have a much bigger life adventure than if we try to control and muddle our way through. Hebrews chapter 11 will show you all the people who lived by faith and what they did. They were not perfect people but people with a heart toward God. That's what qualified them to live by faith, and that's what qualifies us too. How do we develop faith? Listen and hear the voice of God and do what he says.

Miracles and faith work together. As you

know when we pray for others, or ourselves, we are asking for a miracle, as we can't do it in our own ability otherwise we would probably be getting on with it. In the Bible we see Jesus performing lots of miracles and often he will say to the person 'Your faith has made you well.' So we assume that faith and miracles function together. I suppose if we don't have faith that God is capable of doing something we ask, then there is no point in asking in the first place.

In the Old Testament we see God performing miracles and in the New Testament Jesus said 'When you have seen me you have seen the Father.' So Jesus was able to do the same things as God the Father. Jesus also sent out his followers and told them to do miracles, heal the sick and cast out the evil one from those who were oppressed by him (Luke 10) When Jesus was about to die he told his followers 'You will do greater things than I," (John 14:12) He also told them to go into the world and preach about him and the Kingdom of God, and to do the things he had shown them. (Mathew 28:19-20) So today when we know we have God's stamp of approval, we can pray in faith and witness the Kingdom come into our lives and others, bringing goodness.

Over many years I have seen God heal me,

bring finance when I needed, and heal others physically, mentally and spiritually all over the world. So I am writing this so that you will be able to pray and expect miracles to happen in your own life. It takes courage and boldness to follow Jesus in this way, but the Bible teaches us that God has not given us a spirit of timidity but of boldness and a sound mind.

So keep your relationship with God active and adventurous, and be a blessing to whoever God brings your way.

Notes

Notes

Notes

Made in the USA
Charleston, SC
29 August 2014